That little voice in your head

Learning about Your Conscience

Andrew David Naselli
Illustrated by Julie Carter

Acknowledgments

Thanks to friends who graciously offered incisive feedback on this book and helped me communicate more clearly and appropriately. Thanks especially to my wife, Jenni, and our first three daughters, Kara, Gloria, and Emma. Jenni is a master-teacher to children (and earned a degree in Early Childhood Education), and my daughters let me test out the book on them.

Dedication

To my sweet daughter Emma.

About the author

Andrew David Naselli (PhD, Bob Jones University; PhD, Trinity Evangelical Divinity School) is associate professor of New Testament and theology at Bethlehem College & Seminary in Minneapolis and an elder of Bethlehem Baptist Church.

He co-authored the book *Conscience* with J. D. Crowley (Crossway, 2016). He and his wife, Jenni, have been married since 2004, and God has blessed them with four daughters.

A note from the illustrator

Can you find Emma's conscience in the story? That little voice in her head is with her on every page! Every time her conscience changes color, it has a meaning.

This book is given with love to:

_____

from:

_____

Hi, I'm Emma.

I like to eat chocolate.

This is my Mommy. She likes to eat chocolate, too. Dark chocolate. So she keeps a bowl of chocolate chips in the kitchen for special snacks.

One day after lunch, I asked,

"Mommy, may I please have some chocolate chips?"

"No," replied Mommy. "Not now, sweet Emma."

I was not happy. I wanted to eat some chocolate chips. I wanted them so much I decided to sneak some. I waited for Mommy to leave the kitchen. This was my chance. I hurried to the bowl of chocolate chips and scooped a handful out. Then I carefully moved the bowl so that no one would ever know I was there. Those chocolate chips were yummy!

But something happened that bothered me. While I was stealing those chocolate chips, a little voice in my head was telling me,

"Stop. Don't do that. You shouldn't disobey Mommy."

But I wanted the chocolate chips more than I wanted to do what is right. So I did not listen to that voice in my head.

After I ate the yummy chocolate chips, that little voice in my head started talking to me again: "You shouldn't have done that. You shouldn't steal chocolate chips. You shouldn't disobey Mommy. That was bad. You should tell Mommy what you did."

That made me feel sad. I was embarrassed. When I saw Mommy again, I couldn't keep my secret any longer. "Mommy," I cried, "I'm so sorry! I disobeyed you. I ate some chocolate chips."

Mommy looked kindly at me. "I'm sad you disobeyed me, Emma. But I'm glad you finally listened to your conscience and told me about it."

"Conscience? What is my conscience?" I asked.

"It's that little voice in your head that tells you whether something is right or wrong. You can't actually hear that voice. It's the thoughts you think—but not all your thoughts. Not thoughts like 'I'm hungry' or 'I don't want to clean my room.'

"It's the thoughts that say things like 'That is good' and 'That is bad.' It seems like something inside you is telling you what is right and wrong. Sometimes it makes you feel embarrassed."

"Do you have a conscience, too, Mommy?"

"Yes," replied Mommy.

"God gives everyone a conscience. It's a gift."

"A gift?" I asked.

"Yes, it helps us obey God. It helps us not hurt ourselves and other people."

This was a new idea for me. I wanted to think about it some more.

A few days later I was riding my bike outside on the street in front of our home. I love to ride my bike. But this time I lost control and fell onto the street. I scraped the palms of my hands, and my knee was bleeding. Mommy cleaned me up and put a little bandage on my knee. Then she gave me a chocolate popsicle to help me feel better.

While I was eating my treat and feeling better, I asked Mommy some more questions about my conscience—that little voice in my head.

"Mommy, you said my conscience is a gift from God, but it doesn't feel like a gift. My conscience is always telling me how bad I am."

"I know just what you mean, Emma," replied Mommy. "I used to feel the same way."

"What happened?" I asked.

"My conscience used to make me feel embarrassed all the time, but now I have a clear conscience.

My conscience was dirty, and now it is clean."

"How?" I asked.

"Jesus cleaned it. He cleaned it when I turned from my sins and trusted Jesus to save me. Because Jesus died on the cross for me, he cleared away the guilt that my conscience makes me feel. The Bible says the blood of Jesus makes my conscience clean so that I can serve God."

I looked down at my hurt knee. "Blood doesn't clean stuff. So how can blood clean your conscience?" I asked.

"When we say 'Jesus' blood,' we mean 'Jesus' death,'" Mommy explained. "We can have a clean conscience because Jesus died for us."

Then Mommy started singing:

"What can wash away my sin?

Nothing but the blood of Jesus.

What can make me whole again?

Nothing but the blood of Jesus.

What can make my conscience clean?

Nothing but the blood of Jesus."

I asked, "But what happens when your conscience still tells you how bad you are?"

"You are right, Emma. I still sin, so my conscience still tells me I am bad. **But God helps me be sorry for my sin,** and I ask God to forgive me.

"I remember I cannot be good enough on my own. I have a clean conscience only because of Jesus. When Jesus died on the cross for me, he traded his goodness for my sin. So when God looks at me, he sees Jesus' goodness instead of my sin."

Then Mommy started singing from the hymn "Before the Throne of God Above." But instead of saying, "When *Satan* tempts me to despair," she changed it to *conscience* to teach me about the conscience (not because Satan and conscience are the same thing—Satan fights God, but the conscience is a gift from God that can make you feel guilty when you sin):

"When conscience tempts me to despair

And tells me of the guilt within,

Upward I look and see him there

Who made an end of all my sin.

Because the sinless Savior died,

My sinful soul is counted free,

For God, the Just, is satisfied

To look on him and pardon me."

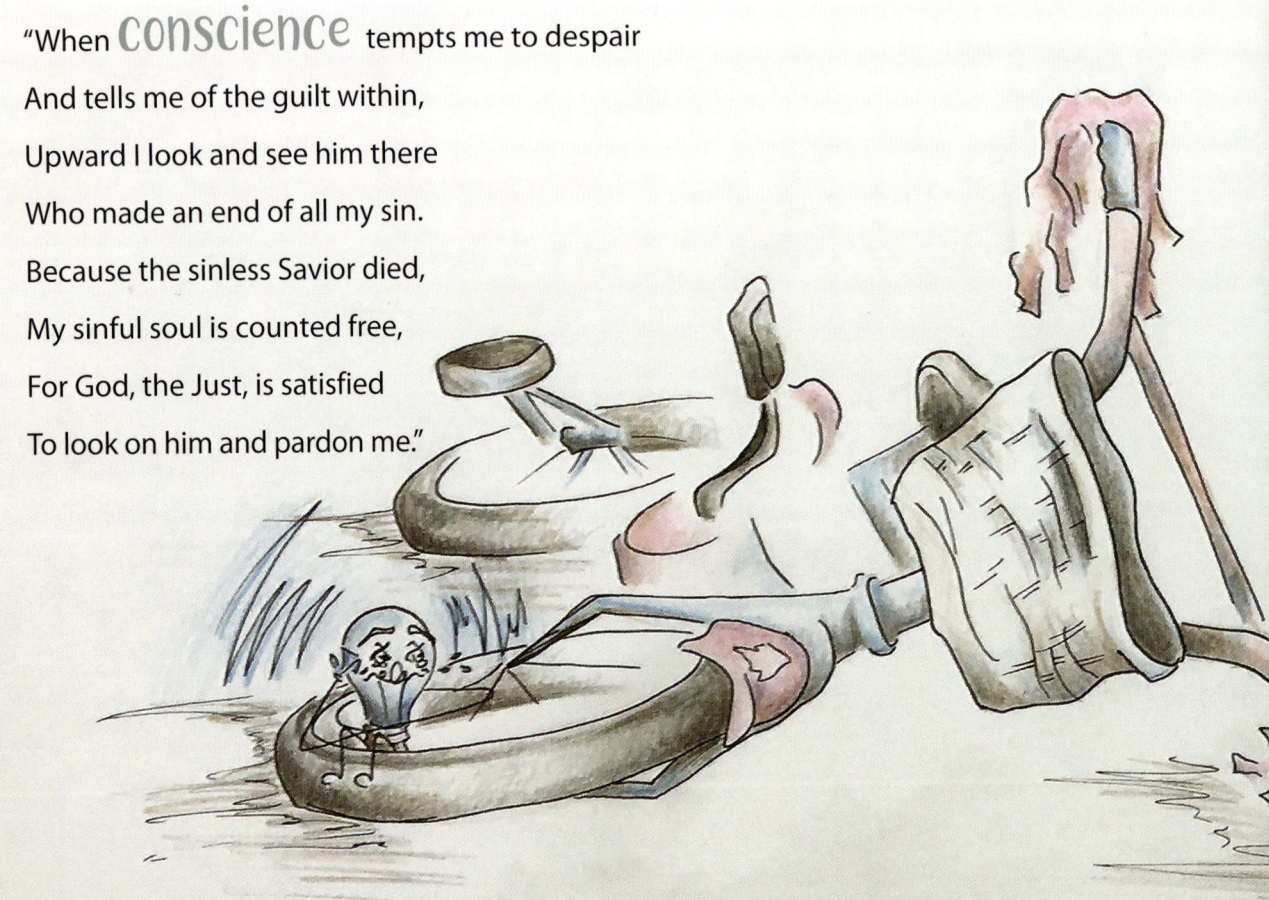

Mommy explained, "Instead of feeling embarrassed and sad, I remember Jesus."

"I remember that **Jesus lived, died, and rose again for me** and that God will save me if I turn from my sins and trust Jesus."

This was a new idea for me. I wanted to think about it some more.

About a week later, I went to my friend Eden's home to play. But **that little voice in my head** kept saying how bad Eden was.

Eden came to the front door wearing her shoes in the house! I thought, "She is being bad for wearing outside shoes inside." (My Mommy and Daddy taught me not to wear shoes in the house.)

Then when we went into Eden's bedroom to play, I saw that she did not make her bed! I thought, "She is being bad for keeping her bed all messy with crumpled sheets and blankets." (My Mommy and Daddy taught me to straighten up my bed after I was done sleeping in it.)

And when Eden's Mommy called us to come eat lunch, Eden did not wash her hands! I thought, "She is being bad for eating without washing her hands first." (My Mommy and Daddy taught me to wash my hands before I eat.)

"Oh, Mommy, you won't believe how bad Eden is," I complained while we were driving home. I told Mommy what Eden did.

After Mommy listened to me, she warned, "Emma, if Eden's parents have different rules than we do, then Eden is not being bad."

I was confused.

Mommy continued, "There is a big difference between Bible rules and family rules. Bible rules are what God says for everybody, and family rules are what parents say for just their kids. The Bible says you should speak truthfully and not lie, but the Bible does not say you must make your bed."

I was still confused.

Mommy continued, "When I tell you to take off your shoes in the house or to make your bed or to wash your hands before you eat, those are our family's rules. That's what Mommy and Daddy think is best for our family. And you must obey those rules because the Bible says,

'Children, obey your parents in the Lord, for this is right.'"

I asked, "So when I'm bigger and live in my own house, do I have to make my bed?"

"No," replied Mommy. "You might want to, but the Bible doesn't say you have to."

I was still a little confused, so Mommy explained, "Emma, each family has its own set of rules that the parents think are best for their family.

"They have rules about all sorts of things that the Bible doesn't talk about.

"So it shouldn't surprise you when your friends have some different family rules.

"That's okay. Everyone should obey the Bible, but families may have some other rules that are not in the Bible."

This was a new idea for me. I wanted to think about it some more.

When Mommy and I arrived home, we made chocolate chip cookies together. I said, "Mommy, I've been thinking about what you said about how Bible rules are different than family rules. But that means my conscience was wrong at Eden's house."

"What do you mean?" asked Mommy.

"My conscience told me Eden was wrong, but Eden wasn't wrong. She was not disobeying the Bible. She was following her family's rules."

"Oh, I see what you mean, Emma," replied Mommy. "Yes, your conscience is not always right. Sometimes it makes you think something is wrong when it's not wrong.

"Sometimes it makes you think something is right when it's not right."

I asked, "You taught me to obey my conscience. But why should I always obey my conscience if it's wrong sometimes?"

"That's a very good question," replied Mommy. "The answer is that you should almost always obey your conscience because that is the safest thing to do.

28

"But sometimes you should help your conscience work better."

"How do I do that?" I asked.

"Very carefully," replied Mommy. "You can help your conscience work better by teaching it what is true, especially what the Bible teaches is true. Teaching your conscience what is true slowly changes what that voice inside your head tells you is right and wrong. The better you understand the Bible, the better your conscience can work."

I asked, "How?

Have you ever helped your conscience work better?"

"Sure," replied Mommy. "Here's one little way I did that. It's not that important, but it seemed really important at the time.

"When I was a little girl, I thought it was wrong for girls to wear jeans. I thought that jeans were only for boys and that only dresses and skirts were for girls."

"But you're wearing jeans right now, Mommy!"

Mommy laughed. "Yes, as you can see, I don't believe that anymore."

"What happened?" I asked.

"I'm not sure where I got the idea that girls shouldn't wear jeans. Maybe it was because all my girl dolls wore dresses. But as I learned more about the Bible, I realized the Bible doesn't teach that girls shouldn't wear jeans."

Mommy explained some more, "The Bible doesn't tell us exactly what to wear or what not to wear. But it does teach us that we should dress in a way that does not selfishly draw attention to ourselves, as if we were wearing a flashing sign that says, 'Everybody look at me!'

"We should dress in a modest way—in a way that is humble and decent and appropriate. And I think I can wear jeans in a modest way."

"So now that little voice in your head doesn't make you feel embarrassed when you wear jeans in a modest way?" I asked.

Mommy replied, "That's right, because—with God's help—I helped my conscience work better. And I was careful not to hurt it."

"How do you hurt your conscience?" I asked.

"By not listening to that little voice in your head when you think it's telling you the right thing. By disobeying it over and over and over. By believing lies instead of the truth of the Bible. You can break your conscience so that it doesn't work the right way."

"That hurts your conscience?" I asked.

Mommy replied, "Yes, it makes it so you might call bad things good and call good things bad."

"Really?" I asked.

"It's sad, but that's how some people think. Some people think it's a good thing for children to dishonor their Mommy and Daddy and to do whatever their heart tells them to do. Some people think it's a bad thing for a Mommy and Daddy to teach their children about Jesus."

My eyes got big, and my eyebrows went high.

Mommy continued, "That is why it is so important to teach your conscience what is true and to help your conscience work better. Then you can call good things good and bad things bad."

Learning about my conscience helps me.

My conscience is that little voice in my head that tells me whether something is right or wrong. My conscience is a gift from God. I should obey my conscience. I can have a clean conscience because of Jesus. (Thank you, Jesus!)

I should not let my conscience say other people are wrong just because their family's rules are different than my family's rules. Bible rules are not the same as family rules.

Teaching my conscience what is true helps it work better.
The better I understand the Bible, the better my conscience can work.

I'd like to think about this some more while eating a snack.

"Mommy, may I please have some chocolate chips?"

Key Bible Verses

"So I always take pains to have a clear conscience toward both God and man."

(Acts 24:16)

"However, not all possess this knowledge. But some, through former association with idols, eat food as really offered to an idol, and their conscience, being weak, is defiled. ... For if anyone sees you who have knowledge eating in an idol's temple, will he not be encouraged, if his conscience is weak, to eat food offered to idols? ... Thus, sinning against your brothers and wounding their conscience when it is weak, you sin against Christ."

(1 Corinthians 8:7, 10, 12)

"... holding faith and a good conscience. By rejecting this, some have made shipwreck of their faith."

(1 Timothy 1:19)

"... how much more will the blood of Christ, who through the eternal Spirit offered himself without blemish to God, purify our conscience from dead works to serve the living God."

(Hebrews 9:14)

"... let us draw near with a true heart in full assurance of faith, with our hearts sprinkled clean from an evil conscience and our bodies washed with pure water."

(Hebrews 10:22)

A Note to Parents

This book targets young children (about ages 4–9). It condenses parts of a book I coauthored with J. D. Crowley: *Conscience: What It Is, How to Train It*, and *Loving Those Who Differ* (Wheaton, IL: Crossway, 2016). We wrote that book for adults, and my daughter Kara, who was eight years old at the time, asked me if I would write a book on the conscience for children. (How could I say No to that?) So if you want to study the conscience in more detail, check out the big-people version.

CHRISTIAN FOCUS PUBLICATIONS

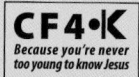

Christian Focus Publications publishes books for adults and children under its four main imprints: Christian Focus, CF4K, Mentor and Christian Heritage. Our books reflect our conviction that God's Word is reliable and Jesus is the way to know him, and live for ever with him. Our children's list includes a Sunday School curriculum that covers pre-school to early teens, and puzzle and activity books. We also publish personal and family devotional titles, biographies and inspirational stories that children will love. If you are looking for quality Bible teaching for children then we have an excellent range of Bible stories and age-specific theological books. From pre-school board books to teenage apologetics, we have it covered!

10 9 8 7 6 5 4 3 2 1

Copyright © 2018 Andrew David Naselli

ISBN: 978-1-5271-0159-3

Published in 2018 by Christian Focus Publications Ltd.

Geanies House, Fearn, Tain, Ross-shire, IV20 1TW, Great Britain

Illustrations by Julie Carter

Design and internal layout: Pete Barnsley (Creative Hoot)

Printed in Malta

"Before the Throne of God Above" 1863 Charitie Lees Smith, 1841–1923.

"Nothing but the Blood" Robert Lowry (1826-1899).

All rights reserved. No part of this publication may be reproduced, stored in a retrieval system, or transmitted, in any form, by any means, electronic, mechanical, photocopying, recording or otherwise without the prior permission of the publisher or a licence permitting restricted copying. In the U.K. such licences are issued by the Copyright Licensing Agency, Saffron House, 6-10 Kirby Street, London, EC1 8TS. www.cla.co.uk Scripture quotations are from The Holy Bible, English Standard Version, copyright © 2001 by Crossway Bibles, a division of Good News Publishers. Used by permission. All rights reserved. ESV Text Edition: 2007.